ELEMENTS OF INTERIOR AND LIGHTFRAME CONSTRUCTION

ELEMENTS OF INTERIOR AND LIGHTFRAME CONSTRUCTION

Katherine S. Ankerson
University of Nebraska—Lincoln

Fairchild Publications, Inc., New York

Executive Editor: Olga T. Kontzias

Assistant Acquisitions Editor: Carolyn Purcell

Editor: Amy Zarkos

Art Director: Adam B. Bohannon

Production Manager: Priscilla Taguer

Editorial Assistant: Suzette Lam

Copy Editor: Chernow Editorial Services, Inc.

Cover and Interior Design: Adam B. Bohannon

CD Developer: Kevin Tedore

CD Voiceover: Elizabeth Hicks

Library of Congress Catalog Card Number: 2002108012

ISBN: 1-56367-255-3

GST R 133004424

Printed in the United States of America

 **DISCLAIMER**

The information in this text is presented as a result of many combined sources, including building and fire codes, manufacturers' literature, common reference books and standards, and the author's professional experience.

Even though the author and publisher believe the information presented to be accurate and complete, they do not warrant it as such. The author and publisher have attempted to make this book as accurate as possible, but do not warrant its suitability for any specific purpose other than as a teaching and learning tool; and they assume no liability for the accuracy and completeness or the application of the work to individual circumstances.

It is the responsibility of users to apply their professional knowledge in the use of the information presented in this book and to consult local building codes and references for specific application information. The reader should consult and follow manufacturers' literature in the selection and application of any specific products.

CONTENTS

PREFACE

The intent of *Elements of Interior and Lightframe Construction* is to promote an understanding of the manner in which actual construction components are assembled, attached, installed, and built. The text and workbook provide an opportunity to understand individual construction components and elements, and their relationship to each other, and the project as a whole. It is written to assist students in gaining an understanding of the components of buildings, their technical relationship to each other, and their implications on design decisions.

Elements of Interior and Lightframe Construction provides information, integrating a variety of learning experiences and approaches to assist the student in internalizing the information. Unlike use of most standard texts, you will not gain all of the information through the text and illustration. The animation and glossary entries are an integral component of the text and must be viewed or experienced, in addition to the reading, to achieve the level of understanding intended. The learning experiences designed and included in this work include the illustrated text, animated glossary, animation and simulation sequence clips, annotated photographs, actual details and drawing examples, and links to various web sites. The workbook is designed to promote a deeper understanding and allow application of the information learned.

The animated glossary contains a written description of the term, an animation or simulation further describing it or its relationship to other components, annotated photographs illustrating the term in the actual construction process, and may include examples of details from construction documents illustrating how the term or element would be shown. The text may be heard by activating the audio component. Adjust volume on your computer as appropriate.

Examples presented herein are done so for illustrative purposes only. It is neither expected nor recommended to use details or design solutions out of context. Each detail is related to a particular condition and must be customized to meet the project requirements. While *Elements of Interior and Lightframe Construction* presents examples of portions of construction documents in a manner that relates the act of creating a construction document to the final result, it is not intended to be a drafting or construction documents text. *Interior Construction Documents*, by author Katherine S. Ankerson, is a text that covers aspects of purpose and creation of construction documents for interior projects.

Code references made within this text are for information only. Refer to the building code and edition adopted in your area for specific requirements. The code in force in the area you are in may have requirements that differ slightly from those cited here.

In every case, when this text suggests you visit construction sites, observe construction, or photograph or sketch certain details or design conditions, it is expected that you will ask for permission prior to doing so. Construction sites can be dangerous places, designers are advised to dress appropriately (including hard hats where required) and be cognizant of activities surrounding them. An active awareness of construction occurring above, below, and around you may prevent accidents.

This text does not pretend to be a source for green and sustainable built environmental research; however, in each chapter, you will find some discussion regarding some or all of the major principles. A design philosophy concerning the global and local environment must be developed by each designer to guide his or her decision-making processes. Awareness of some of the green issues with various materials and processes of construction with regard to sustainability should be supplemented by more in-depth review and analysis.

When opening the CD-ROM for the first time, you are encouraged to check your system for the minimum program requirements. Installation of required players are provided on the CD-ROM. Experience the tutorial, an active demonstration of the features contained therein and how to use them.

Acknowledgements

A unique combination of experience and people has shaped this digital textbook. My architectural education, architectural and interior design practice, and construction experience have given me a breadth of experience and knowledge to draw upon. Living and teaching in various parts of this country have imparted a wealth of examples to use. I extend my appreciation to students at Washington State University, Radford University, and the University of Nebraska, whose quest for understanding, knowledge, and excellence have been a constant source of inspiration.

The digital seed was planted by Kim Singhrs, professor at Washington State University, through a wonderful course teaming graduate architecture with computer science students to explore high-end computer programs including Wavefront and Alias, initiating possibilities of this media as a teaching and learning tool.

My colleagues in interior design education have provided both encouragement and inspiration. Colleagues associated with other academic fields, yet with a profound interest in tapping the power of technology as an educational tool have been a stimulus, and I have learned much from them.

Kevin Tedore has been a joy to work with on this project. He has transformed my sketches, images, drawings, and ideas and given them an active digital life. Thank you to those in the profession who have shared images and drawings for this text.

Mary McGarry, Olga Kontzias, and Amy Zarkos at Fairchild Books are an author's dream. I would also like to thank the following reviewers, and fellow instructors, for their insightful and helpful comments and suggestions: Glenn Edgar Currie, Art Institute of Pittsburgh; Francis C. Morigi, Syracuse University; Luann Nissen, University of Nevada—Reno; Jill Pable, California State University—Sacramento; Marty Plumbo, University of Cincinnati; Christopher Priest, Minnesota State University; Roberto J. Rengel, University of Wisconsin—Madison; and Patricia Viard, Western Michigan University.

Finally, I wish to extend my acknowledgement and appreciation to my family for their support. Through the encouragement, pride, and support of my husband John and children, Jason, Matt, and Kelsey, this work has been nurtured from seed to a healthy existence. They have shared the vision.

ELEMENTS OF INTERIOR AND LIGHTFRAME CONSTRUCTION

CHAPTER ONE

Residential and Commercial Construction Methods

Each building system used, whether for a residential or a commercial building type, carries its own unique characteristics. The structural systems forming each system of construction have a bearing on the size and flexibility of spaces that may be created within the building. Remember that no matter the size or type of building, gravity has a huge influence in design. Loads that may be applied to the building must follow a path all the way into the ground.

Building codes view types of construction as a major factor for many allowances and requirements. The 2000 International Building Code specifies nine distinct types of construction under five major categories. Type I and II construction (including IA, IB, IIA, and IIB) are those in which the structural frame, walls, floors, and roof are created of noncombustible materials. The differences in the A and B qualifiers following the type of construction relate to added protection (in the form of fireproofing) or the types of materials allowed within the building for bearing walls.

Type III construction (including IIIA and IIIB) requires exterior walls to be noncombustible, but allows combustible materials elsewhere in the construction. Type III construction is typically found in urban locations where buildings are directly next to each other and, in fact, where they may share exterior walls. Type III construction is used to ensure that a fire in one building will not affect the adjoining building.

Type IV construction is also known as heavy timber construction. Type IV construction utilizes large timber members for columns, floor framing, and roof framing with the large timber composed of either glue-laminated pieces or sawn lumber. Heavy timber construction relies on the size of the wood for its effectiveness in thwarting the effects of a fire. Large sizes of wood, when subject to fire, are charred on the exposed surfaces. This charring slows the progress of the fire and basically insulates the interior core of the wood. Keeping this in mind, it is easy to understand why the timber must be sawn lumber or glue-laminated pieces rather than built-up sections of dimensional lumber. Built-up sections would allow fire to penetrate into the center of the wood more easily; thus, they would not afford the same level of protection as heavy timber.

Type V construction (including VA and VB) allows any material otherwise allowed by the International Building Code to be used for structural frame, walls, floor, and roof. The materials must meet all other applicable requirements of the code. Lightframe construction is included in the Type V construction category. Once again, the A and B designations refer to the level of fire protection on the structure or other components. The A designation refers to a one-hour protection on necessary elements, whereas the B designation has no requirements for protection other than that of the materials themselves.

Building codes also base decisions on the type of occupancy determined to be in the building. The type of occupancy affects nearly every decision made in the code.

Common building practices vary throughout North America. Labor forces may be more familiar with certain materials or methods of construction. Cost savings are realized when designers and architects acknowledge the common practices in particular areas. In some areas, the labor force may be in high demand; thus, labor costs will be significant on projects. With the realization of this (and with a budget in mind), you may design solutions that rely less on hours of labor and more on the choice of materials utilized.

Visit construction sites within your area that are primarily conventional lightframe construction. Observe that the predominant framing materials used are wood, whether dimensional lumber, composite wood materials, or trusses. You will occasionally see a steel beam used for support of floors. This will be the case when an uninterrupted area is desired because the steel beam will span further than a comparable wood beam. (Columns can be further apart.)

As you tour buildings under construction, notice the relative sizes and volumes of space. Limitations are sometimes based more on precon- ceived notions of housing and economics than building system imposition. Be prepared to discuss observed spaces with your perception for the limi- tations or lack thereof (i.e. materials used, functional requirements, and building systems). Use sketches and notes on the following pages to describe your observations.

Lightframe Construction Observations: Sketch 1

NOTES

Lightframe Construction Observations: Sketch 2

NOTES

Record any questions you have as a result of your observations in Sketches 1 and 2:

_____

_____

_____

_____

Lightframe Construction Observations: Detail Sketches 3 and 4

NOTES

_____

_____

_____

_____

_____

_____

_____

NOTES

_____

_____

_____

_____

_____

_____

_____

Focus on connections or intersections in Sketches 3 and 4.

Record any questions you may have as a result of your observations in Sketches 3 and 4:

_____

_____

_____

_____

_____

To learn more about conventional residential building materials and methods for new and existing buildings, visit any of these journals:

Builder Magazine

Journal of Lightframe Construction

Old House Journal

How does what you have seen in the journal(s) relate to what you have seen in person and the sketches and observations you have made?

_____

_____

_____

_____

_____

_____

_____

_____

Many old warehouse structures are constructed of heavy timber construction. Many communities contain old warehouses that have been renovated for use as restaurants, retail establishments, or offices. Visit old warehouses in your area (if there aren't any, look at architecture and interior design periodicals for examples of renovated structures). Notice the size of columns, the size of beams, and other structural elements. Observe the relative column spacings (how far columns are from each other in both directions). In the following spaces, sketch and make notes regarding the relative size and location relationships of columns in the heavy timber example you have found (create plan and perspective sketches).

Heavy Timber Construction Observations: Plan with descriptive notes

NOTES

Heavy Timber Construction Observations: Perspective sketch

NOTES

Observe commercial structures in your area that are under construction. If there are no buildings currently under construction, visit a completed building while viewing a set (or an abbreviated set) of architectural drawings. (Building departments have these plans on record for recently completed buildings. Facility-planning departments at universities maintain plans for all university buildings.) Discover where the structural columns are placed. Examine the manner in which walls or other space divisions respond to the column layout. (For example, do walls consistently meet the columns along an edge? Do the walls meet columns at the centerline? Are walls held away from columns?)

———————————————————————————————
———————————————————————————————
———————————————————————————————
———————————————————————————————
———————————————————————————————

Are there spaces that contain a number of columns within a particular room? Does this affect the intended function of the space?

———————————————————————————————
———————————————————————————————
———————————————————————————————
———————————————————————————————
———————————————————————————————

Discussion

Be prepared to discuss the differences you observe in the heavy timber building type as opposed to conventional lightframe construction. Be prepared to contrast differences in commercial construction observed with both the heavy timber building and the conventional lightframe construction buildings. Are there limitations imposed by the general building systems used in the buildings visited?

———————————————————————————————
———————————————————————————————
———————————————————————————————
———————————————————————————————
———————————————————————————————

Do these limitations affect the way you would approach space planning in these building types?

_____

_____

_____

_____

Assignment

From current design periodicals (within the current two-year period), select a project that intrigues you. Identify from the information given the construction systems used in the project (selecting a published project with the plans shown in addition to photographs of finished spaces is highly desirable). Assess the impact of the construction system used on the design of spaces contained within the building. In 250–500 words, discuss your findings and analysis. Supplement the written work with at least one analytical diagram (this could be an overlay of a plan or section drawing) and at least one image that best describes the finished space. Incorporate the images into the text in the appropriate locations to support your observations and analysis; cite the sources of the images. Submit a copy of the article you have used as a basis for your inquiry.

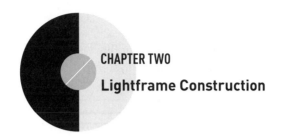

CHAPTER TWO

Lightframe Construction

Lightframe construction refers to an entire system of construction composed of wood products that work together to create the structure of a building. Components of lightframe construction include wood studs, trusses, joists, rafters, plates, and all of the accessories necessary to create a complete structure.

Lightframe construction relies on the repetitive spacing of wood members for distribution of loads. Equal and repetitive spacing of framing members correspond to the modular nature of sheet materials such as plywood and gypsum drywall commonly used as sheathing and finish materials.

Lightframe construction is currently used for the majority of single- and two-family residential projects in the United States. Multifamily residential and small commercial projects up to three stories in height are also often created with lightframe construction. Divisions of trades involved in a lightframe project often include foundation or concrete subcontractors; framing subcontractors; plumbing; electrical; heating, ventilating, and air conditioning subcontractors; finish carpenters; and roofing subcontractors.

This chapter is divided into four sections regarding lightframe construction: Foundation Systems, Floor Systems, Wall Systems, and Roof Systems. The principles and terminology of construction presented in the chapter are important in understanding lightframe construction as well as other types of construction discussed later. After reading each section on the CD-ROM, exploring each of the glossary entries, and exploring web links, answer the following questions and prepare the following assignments.

Foundation Systems

1. From the given drawings located on the CD-ROM, identify the indicated parts of a foundation system.

A. _____

B. _____

C. _____

2. Search the drawings included on the CD-ROM for information included to answer the following questions:

A. What type of foundation system do the drawings indicate that this structure contains? (Slab on grade, crawl space, basement)

_____

B. How does the foundation system in this structure connect to the framing above? Is the framing directly above the foundation system a floor system or a wall system?

_____

_____

C. What is the thickness of the foundation wall shown for this structure?

_____

D. Are there any isolated footings located on the drawings for this structure?

_____

3. Foundation systems are typically constructed of poured concrete or concrete masonry units for conventional lightframe construction. Alternative methods of creating foundations also exist; these might include the use of treated wood or various insulation forms. Describe with sketch and words any other foundation systems you have observed:

Foundation System Observations: Sketch 1

NOTES

_____

_____

_____

_____

_____

_____

_____

_____

4. Search periodicals and web sites for alternative methods and materials used in residential foundation construction. Concentrate on one alternative system and describe that system in a written (250–500 words) and graphic format. In your written work, discuss the materials used, relative advantages and disadvantages of the system, and the extent to which this system is currently being utilized. Include a minimum of one image that graphically describes the system. Be prepared to discuss your findings with the class.

Floor Systems

1. From the given drawings located on the CD-ROM, identify the indicated parts of a floor system.

A. _____

B. _____

C. _____

2. Search the drawings included on the CD-ROM for information included to answer the following questions:

A. What materials are used as floor joists? (Dimensional lumber, composite lumber, truss systems?)

_____

B. What is the overall depth of the floor system, not including any ceiling material shown?

_____

C. Are any beams included in the floor system? If so, of what material is (are) the beam(s) constructed?

_____

3. Search periodicals and web sites for alternative methods and materials used in residential floor construction. Concentrate on one alternative system that consciously focuses on green or sustainable practices and describe that system in a written (250–500 words) and graphic format. In your written work, discuss the materials used as well as the features that set the system apart as a sustainable building practice. Be sure to cite advantages and disadvantages of the system. Include a minimum of one image that graphically describes the system. Be prepared to discuss your findings with the class.

4. If you live in a home with an unfinished basement or have ready access to one, go into that space and look at the framing for the floor system above. What size are the floor joists?

_____

Are there beams? If so, what are the dimensions and how far do they span?

_____

If you can see the subfloor, describe the materials that compose it:

_____

_____

Wall Systems
1. From the given drawings located on the CD-ROM, identify the indicated parts of a wall system.

A. _____

B. _____

C. _____

D. _____

2. Search the drawings included on the CD-ROM for information included to answer the following questions:

A. What dimension are the studs used for the load-bearing walls of this building? From the information shown, can you determine the stud size and spacing of other interior or exterior walls? Why do you think the load-bearing walls are called out specifically?

_____

_____

_____

_____

_____

B. How does the wall system in this structure connect to the floor structure below?

_____

_____

_____

_____

_____

Exterior walls for conventional lightframe construction are typically constructed with dimensional lumber studs. Alternative methods of creating exterior walls also exist, employing various framing techniques or different building materials.

3. Search periodicals and web sites for alternative methods and materials used in residential wall construction. Concentrate on one alternative system and describe that system in a written (250–500 words) and graphic format. In your written work, discuss the materials used, relative advantages and disadvantages of the system, and the extent this system is currently being utilized. Include a minimum of one image that graphically describes the system. (As an alternative, create a print advertisement for the system you researched.) Be prepared to discuss your findings with the class.

4. Create an axonometric drawing of framing for an interior wall containing a framed door opening. The wall is to be shown framed with 2x4s spaced at 24" o.c. Label each of the components of the framing.

Axonometric of Wall Framing: Sketch 2

Roof Systems

1. From the given drawings located on the CD-ROM, identify the indicated parts of the roof system.

A. _____

B. _____

C. _____

D. _____

E. _____

F. _____

2. Search the drawings included on the CD-ROM for information included to answer the following questions:

A. What types of roof systems do the drawings indicate that this structure contains? (Rafter, truss, combination?)

_____

B. Are there any dormers located on the roof?

_____

C. What is the slope of the roof?

_____

D. Are any skylights located in the roof system? How many?

_____

3. Search periodicals and web sites for alternative methods and materials used in residential roof construction. Focus on one practice, method, or material that exemplifies sustainability. Describe that practice, method or material in a written (250 words) and graphic format. In your written work, discuss the materials used and the features that cause this practice to be sustainable, as well as the extent to which this system is currently being utilized. What might cause this material or system to become common practice? Include a minimum of one image that graphically describes your choice. Be prepared to discuss your findings with the class.

4. Observe construction sites of lightframe construction. Describe with annotated section drawings on the following page, two different methods of creating a cathedral ceiling within a living space. Be specific in the representation of framing.

Cathedral Ceiling Framing Method 1: Sketch 3

Cathedral Ceiling Framing Method 2: Sketch 4

CHAPTER THREE

Commercial Construction

Most nonresidential buildings utilize a building system other than lightframe construction. This is often due to the number of stories in the building or the fire-resistive requirements by building codes. Other times, it is due to local practices or availability of materials. This chapter discusses common commercial building elements as well as their relationship to each other. Read and review the material on the CD-ROM prior to engaging in the following exercises.

Structural Systems

The structural system in a building provides the general skeleton designed to withstand all of the loads placed on the building, whether those loads are a result of external factors such as wind, snow, or earthquakes, or due to internal loads such as the weight of materials, people, and equipment. Columns, beams, walls, and trusses may all be integral components of the structural system. A variety of materials may be found acting as the structural system. In commercial construction these materials typically revolve around various forms of concrete, steel, and heavy timber.

1. Peruse current architectural and interior design periodicals to find examples of various structural systems used within the projects. Identify two buildings with very different structural systems. Document and describe the structural system for each project in both a written and graphic format. Determine the building's use and discuss the relevancy of the structural system to the use. Does the structural system seem to support the intended use in terms of spatial concerns?

_____

_____

_____

_____

_____

_____

_____

_____

_____

_____

2. Are there any areas of the buildings whose use is enhanced by the particular structural system or seemingly hampered by particular components of the structural system?

_____

_____

_____

_____

_____

_____

_____

_____

_____

_____

_____

_____

_____

Floor Systems

Commercial floor systems can be diverse; their design depends on several issues in the building design process, including the load to be carried, the overall structural system designed for the building, flexibility, and, of course, cost. Solutions are available in floor systems from those that can span a great distance from one support to another support to those requiring short spans and close supports.

1. On the following diagram, identify the elements of commercial floor systems indicated:

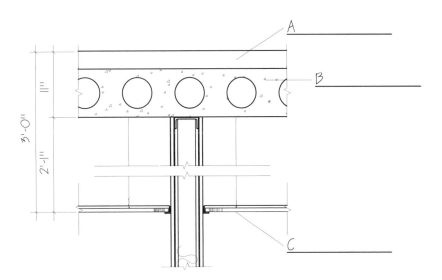

Commecial Floor Exercise 1 A-C

Why might the floor system shown be utilized rather than other floor systems?

_____

_____

_____

_____

2. Search the drawings included on the CD-ROM for information included to answer the following questions. Support your observations with information gained from published sources. Include graphics where necessary to fully explain your conclusions.

A. What type of floor system do the drawings indicate that this structure contains?

_____

_____

_____

B. From what is the subfloor constructed? What is the thickness of the subfloor?

_____

_____

_____

C. What is the overall thickness of the floor system shown on the drawings (not including ceiling materials)?

_____

_____

_____

3. Of the typical commercial systems utilized for floor systems, briefly describe the system that uses the most sustainable practices.

_____

_____

_____

_____

_____

_____

Wall Systems

Interior walls in commercial construction may be assembled with many materials; by far the most common construction is that of light-gauge steel framing with drywall on each side. Other wall systems may utilize concrete masonry units (usually where fire ratings need to be quite high), glass block, or wood studs. The actual construction of the wall is dependent on such design determinants as the loading placed on the wall, the height of the wall, the visual characteristics of the wall, code requirements of fire-resistive qualities, and acoustical considerations.

1. From the given drawing of a typical wall meeting a suspended ceiling system (located on the CD-ROM), identify the indicated parts of the light-gauge steel wall system.

A. _____

B. _____

C. _____

D. _____

2. Observe walls in commercial buildings you are in. Select one wall and describe the finish material.

_____

_____

_____

Describe how the wall meets the floor. If base trim is present, describe it in terms of size, material, and finish.

_____

_____

_____

_____

_____

Describe the manner in which the wall meets the ceiling.

_____

_____

_____

_____

_____

How might the wall be framed behind the finish materials?

_____

_____

_____

_____

Ceiling Systems

There are three major classifications of ceiling systems, based on their attachment to the structure above, used in commercial construction. The ceiling system can be the actual exposed structure, including mechanical and electrical systems. The ceiling can be directly attached to the structure, or the ceiling can be suspended from the structure above, providing a plenum space. Decisions regarding the classification of ceiling systems generate from aesthetic considerations of the structural system, contribution of the ceiling system to the overall design, code considerations of fire-resistive qualities, and desired integration of lighting and other building systems.

1. From the given drawing of a typical commercial ceiling (located on the CD-ROM), identify the indicated parts of the suspended ceiling system.

A. _____

B. _____

C. _____

D. _____

2. Search periodicals and web sites for alternative methods and materials used to construct or install commercial ceiling systems. Concentrate on one alternative system and describe it in a written (250–500 words) and graphic format. In your written work, discuss the materials used, relative advantages and disadvantages of the system, and the extent this system is currently being utilized. Include a minimum of one image that graphically describes the system. Be prepared to discuss your findings with the class.

3. Describe the most interesting ceiling treatment you have observed.

_____

_____

_____

_____

_____

In what sort of space was this ceiling located?

_____

_____

_____

Describe how lighting or other systems were included in this system.

_____

_____

_____

_____

What height was the ceiling from the floor?

_____

_____

_____

_____

Was the entire ceiling the same height?

_____

_____

_____

_____

If yes, why do you believe the ceiling was created at a uniform height?

_____

_____

_____

_____

_____

If not, explain where the ceiling varies in height. (For instance, is it over certain functional areas?)

_____

_____

_____

_____

_____

Does the ceiling meet the walls? Describe.

_____

_____

_____

_____

_____

CHAPTER FOUR

Stairs, Ramps, and Floor Level Changes

Stairs, ramps, and railings have been incorporated in buildings throughout history for both symbolic and functional purposes. Floor level changes have evolved in this country to a state of comfort and safety for all occupants, suggested by design guidelines and regulated by building codes.

Many factors must be considered in the design of a stair system. Aesthetic features play an important role, both in terms of visual perceptions, and in a tactile sense. Material use and the actual form of the treads and risers contribute to this aesthetic, as does the design of the railing system.

The dimensions of the stairs, both in terms of individual treads and risers, and also in terms of the width of the stair, plays an important role in the users' impressions of the overall space. A narrow stair may seem very functional, while a wide stair may conjure images of grandeur. Likewise, the height between landings affects users' perceptions of the space. Pushing the limits of code allowances for height limitations between landings may create a stair that looks and feels oppressive.

The stair run shape is also important in an aesthetic and certainly functional manner. Through incorporation of a turn in the stair, designers can control where the user enters a space on an adjacent floor, increasing or decreasing occupants' anticipations of that space. Ascending or descending a stair can be an event with its own significance, accentuated by the stair shape. From a practical viewpoint, moving furniture or other large objects up or down a stair with tight turns can be quite challenging.

Codes regulate several features of stairs. Overall maximum heights and minimum widths and the necessity and placement of handrails are some features thus affected. Codes strictly regulate variations in stair riser heights and in tread depths within the same stair, as a variation creates a danger to users in terms of tripping hazard.

Ramps have also been used throughout history, especially when wheeled vehicles or other apparatus need to traverse vertical distances. Ramps are regulated by building codes for safety, just as stairs are. Maximum slope, landing dimensions, and surface treatment are each factors addressed by building and accessibility codes. As far as codes are concerned, ramps may replace stairs in a design, but the opposite is certainly not true. When a ramp is required, a stair will not suffice in its place.

Railing systems contribute to the design and impact of stairs and ramps and to any location where people must be protected from adjacent vertical height differences. Two main systems of rails are distinguished as handrails and guardrails. Handrails are gripped as one uses a stair or ramp system. Guardrails protect from height differences. Both are often included on the same railing system design.

Building codes regulate minimum height for railing systems, as well as the maximum space allowed between elements in the system (this prevents people, especially children, and objects from inadvertently falling through). The grip of a handrail is similarly addressed through the codes, as are spacings of handrails from walls or other surfaces.

Observe stairs, ramps, floor level changes, and railings in buildings close to you. Determine the functional intentions of the system. While this may seem obvious at first blush, go the next step in consideration by addressing each of the factors affecting design mentioned earlier. Travel on the system, let your body experience the ascending and descending nature, and allow your hand to run along the handrail. Consider the aesthetic contribution of the system to the entire space or building. Is the contribution congruous?

_____

_____

_____

_____

_____

_____

Does it reinforce the building design intent?

_____

_____

_____

_____

_____

_____

Is there a particular portion of the system that contributes more strongly?
Describe.

_____

_____

_____

_____

Is there a particular portion that seems out of place? Explain.

_____

_____

_____

_____

_____

_____

Is the system used as a point of emphasis? How?

_____

_____

_____

_____

_____

_____

Be prepared to discuss your observations and perceptions with the class.

General Considerations

1. From the following drawing, identify the indicated elements of a stair system.

A. _____

B. _____

C. _____

D. _____

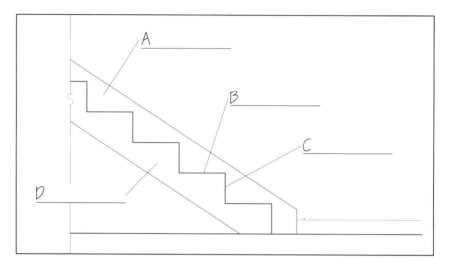

Stair Exercise 1 A–D

2. For the following scenarios, calculate the tread and riser dimensions and answer the associated queries (show your process):

Scenario One: The stairway serving from the first to second floor of a two-story office building must span a vertical distance of 12'6".

A. What is an appropriate riser height for this stairway?

_____

_____

B. What will the tread depth be for this stairway?

_____

C. Are any intermediate landings required on this stairway?

_____

Scenario Two: The stairway serving two floors of a single-family residence must span a vertical distance of 9'0".

A. Are any intermediate landings required on this stairway?

_____

B. What is an appropriate riser height for this stairway?

_____

C. What will the tread depth be for this stairway?

_____

3. Select one element of a stair, ramp, floor level change, or railing system (i.e., nosings, baluster, intersection of baluster and tread, etc.) and photograph or sketch a minimum of five different design approaches to this element from current print periodicals or actual buildings. Circle the area of interest and describe in 25–50 words the unique characteristics of each. Compile onto the following pages for submission.

Design Approach 1: Sketch 1

UNIQUE CHARACTERISTICS

_____
_____
_____
_____
_____
_____
_____

Design Approach 2: Sketch 2

UNIQUE CHARACTERISTICS

Design Approach 3: Sketch 3

UNIQUE CHARACTERISTICS

_____

_____

_____

_____

_____

_____

_____

Design Approach 4: Sketch 4

UNIQUE CHARACTERISTICS

Design Approach 5: Sketch 5

UNIQUE CHARACTERISTICS

Wood Stairs and Railings

1. For the following drawing of a wood stair system, identify the indicated elements as well as what the typical material might be.

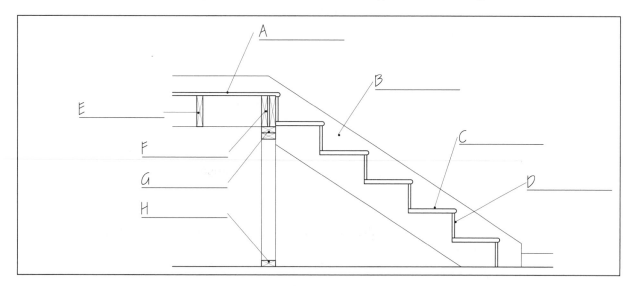

A. _____

B. _____

C. _____

D. _____

E. _____

F. _____

G. _____

H. _____

2. Select two examples (one of contemporary or modern design, one of historic or traditional design) of wood stairs from actual examples found in existing buildings, or from periodicals. Provide a comparative analysis of the stairs in both written (250 words) and graphic format. Be sure to include an analysis of relative proportions, materials used, finishes used, and decorative aspects or applied ornamentation.

Metal Stairs and Railings

1. For the following two section drawings of a metal stair system, answer the following questions:

A. What is the height of each riser?

_____

B. What type of structure is used for the landing construction?

_____

_____

_____

C. What material are the stringers composed of?

_____

D. What is the maximum clear distance between pipe railings?

_____

E. Why is the top rail continuous even though the stair changes direction?

_____

_____

_____

_____

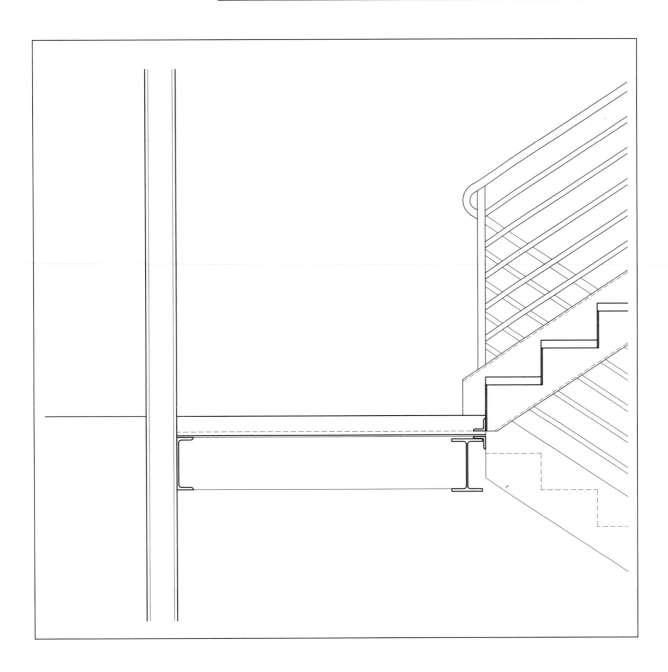

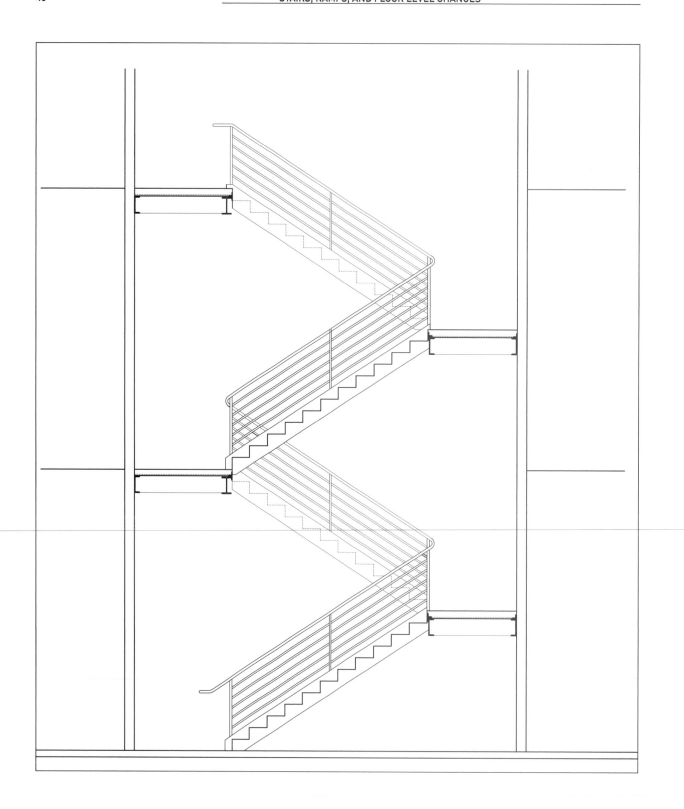

2. Select two examples of interior metal stairs and railings from buildings in your area. Document the stairs with photographs. Note the type of space in which each is located. For each of the examples, capture the apparent design intent of each stair in approximately 100 words. In an additional 100–200 words, compare and contrast the examples in terms of area of use and materials used for treads, risers, stringers, and railing systems. Examine and discuss how connections are made. Present the photographs, descriptions, and comparative analysis in an 8½" × 11" format.

Ramps and Railings

1. Identify one excellent example of a ramp and associated railings from a current periodical. On one 8½" × 11" white sheet include a visual image of the example (traced or copied), identify the major components of the system, and describe the materials used in the ramp system for the railings as well as the ramp and landing surfaces. Be prepared to discuss your example, including benefits and drawbacks of this particular design.

2. Describe in detail three distinct material choices appropriate for ramp surfaces.
Material A:

_____

_____

_____

Material B:

_____

_____

_____

Material C:

_____

_____

_____

3. Using the following scenario and template, sketch the section of a ramp system. Label the parts, indicating dimensions where necessary.

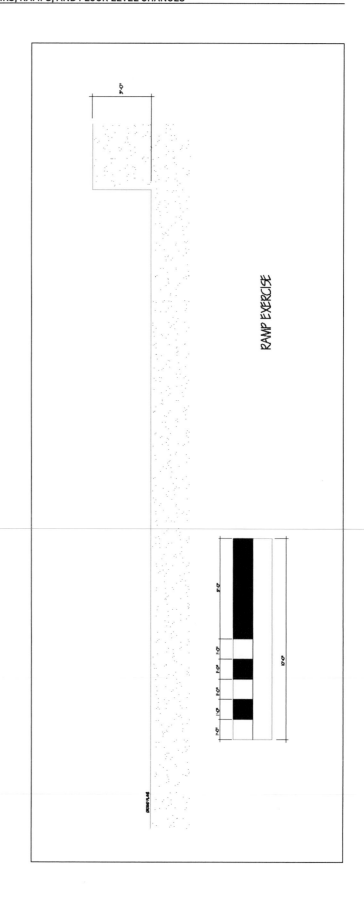

RAMP EXERCISE

Other Railing Systems

1. Find two examples of "other" railing systems used in building interiors from current periodicals. Sketch a section through each of the railing sections to illustrate how it might be constructed. Be sure to show a connection to the surface or structure below. Describe each of the examples with notes to explain the materials and connections used.

Railing System 1: Sketch 6

Railing System 2: Sketch

2. Locate an example of using a half-wall as a guardrail. Annotate sketches or photographs of the conditions at the top termination of the half-wall. Be prepared to share and discuss your findings with the class.

Sketches or Photograph:

CHAPTER FIVE

Doors and Glazing

Openings in a wall may be created for passage of people or objects or for visual and/or acoustical access. Openings are distinguished through their shape, sense of transparency or opaqueness, framing, and what lies within, whether a door, glazing, other material, or nothing at all. Openings contribute to the overall design of a space in a major aesthetic and functional manner.

When outfitted with a door, the opening creates a sense of enclosure, yet access, and can portray the character of the space. As a design element, doors separate spaces while providing a sense of security, identity, and motion. Doors may be heavy or light in visual and actual weight. This may contribute to a sense of privacy or separation (a door, light in appearance, carries the perception of acoustical transparency, thus a low degree of privacy). There may be a sense of visual transparency with doors. It is a complex task to design and detail a door; design intentions must be clear, as there are a number of decisions based on these intentions.

Doors are available in a variety of qualities, materials, widths, thicknesses, fire ratings, profiles, and manners of operation. Selection of individual attributes depends on the proposed use and location, desired appearance, required fire rating, and cost. Standard sizes (heights, widths, and thicknesses) are available and most commonly used, but doors can be custom-designed and fabricated as well.

Considerations in the selection of doors for interior projects are many. A door often creates the first impression both visually and in a tactile sense of the style and quality of the interior. Few components of the interior environment are touched as much as the door and associated hardware. Attention to tactile qualities is a significant consideration. Doors may be designed or selected to accentuate an opening or to blend in with a wall surface. Consideration of durability and frequency of use alludes to decisions regarding operation and finish. Acoustical considerations regarding the door itself generally refer to the mass of the door. The door selection for acoustical considerations is only one part of the equation; the frame type, installation, and hardware selection play equal roles in acoustical performance.

Glazing on a project may be found in several locations—in exterior walls as windows or curtain walls, on the roof as skylights, in interior walls as relites or entire walls, and in doors and sidelites. Glazing allows light to enter, has the potential to provide view in and out, capture sunlight, frame views, extend interior space out, or extend exterior space in. Issues of heat gain or loss, visual and acoustical privacy, view, security, and code considerations all enter into the design decisions regarding glazing.

Building and life safety codes articulate specific requirements for location, type, and size of glazing. When we keep in mind that each of the codes has the primary purpose of safeguarding the health, life, and safety of building occupants, the variety and comprehensive nature of requirements for glazing seem reasonable.

Frames encase an opening and allow movement of the door or window. Frames are selected on the basis of desired finished appearance; code requirements; hardware and security needs; and specific door, glazing, or opening requirements. Specific frames may also be selected in part based on the installation method necessary for the wall opening. Determination of the required fire rating for the door assembly is one of the largest factors when selecting the frame. Security and durability are important considerations that determine not only the material of the frame, but the finish and anchorage of it as well.

Selection of door hardware is governed by the required function, operating characteristics and constraints, durability, appearance, code requirements, accessibility, security, and special considerations.

Hardware for door operation can be divided into the categories of "operation," "control," and "accessories." Within the general category of "operation" fall hinges, pivots, and closers. The general category of "control" includes latches, locking devices, panic hardware, doorknobs and lever handles, door pulls and push plates. "Accessories" include such items as kick plates, escutcheons, acoustic seals, stops, and bumpers.

Doors

Many different doors are used in residential and commercial construction. Selection of doors occurs at a design level while considering symbolic as well as functional issues. Investigation of the construction, materials, sizes, and typical uses of various doors will require you to become familiar with a variety of terms and relationships that will be located within the chapter.

1. Individually or as a team, find as many *different* examples of interior doors as possible within one hour. Photograph or sketch the doors, indicating the location within the building, material(s), and operation. Describe aesthetic as well as functional characteristics of each door. Be prepared to discuss your findings with the class.

2. Visit a local home improvement or lumber store to investigate and record the possibilities in selections for a paint-grade, wood, swinging door. Select a common size and record price information. Supplement your investigation with an online search for similar products. Record your findings in a tabular form with columns for "brand or manufacturer," "size," "material," "style," "price," and "special features." Be prepared to turn in your work and to discuss your findings with the class.

3. As a scenario, you are designing a commercial space with code requirements for a 36" wide, 20-minute door ratings. You wish to have maple doors with a transparent finish. Peruse printed product guides or online to find a minimum of three choices for these doors. Answer the following questions:
A. How can you be certain the 20-minute rating is accomplished for each door?
B. What is the thickness of each door?
C. What options are available for each door found with regard to grain pattern?

Glazing

1. Two scenarios of window elevations are included on the CD-ROM, labeled 1A and 1B. From the information given, determine whether these windows are allowable egress windows for sleeping areas. If they are not allowable egress windows, discuss reasons why.

A. _____

_____

_____

B. _____

_____

_____

2. For the glazing elevations shown on the CD-ROM, labeled 2A and 2B, determine which (if any) of the glazing panels need to contain safety glazing. List the panels that must contain safety glazing below.

A. _____

_____

_____

B. _____

_____

3. Measure the window(s) in your current sleeping room in your present residence. Represent the measurements in an elevation sketch on the following sheet, including the floor and ceiling lines. On the sketch, note specific elements of the measurements that determine whether the window(s) meet the requirements listed in the chapter as a part of the 2000 International Building Code as egress windows.

Sleeping Room Elevation Sketch: Sketch 1

NOTES

Frame Types

Frames are selected on the basis of desired finished appearance; code requirements; hardware and security needs; and specific door, glazing, or opening requirements. Frames may be of many materials; the most common are wood, steel, and aluminum. Specific frames may also be selected in part based on the installation method necessary to the wall opening, as well as the contribution of the frame to fire-resistive qualities of the opening.

1. On the following page, illustrate three variations of a wood doorframe and associated trim by completing a section through a jamb (show at least 3" of the door as well). Show each of the variations to scale and label each of the components.

2. Identify examples of two different frame types used in an interior location in local buildings. Draw a sketch and note on the sketch measurements of the various components of the frame, as well as the thickness of the door or glazing included within. Take a photograph of each frame to include with your work. (*Caution*: If selecting frames from local, privately owned buildings, you must gain permission prior to taking photographs.) In a written (250 words) and graphic format, describe each of the frames (including the general location of each) and point out differences between them. Suggest reasons why the designer may have selected each type of frame for the particular use. Do you agree with the selection and use of each? Why or why not? Be prepared to share and discuss your examples with the class.

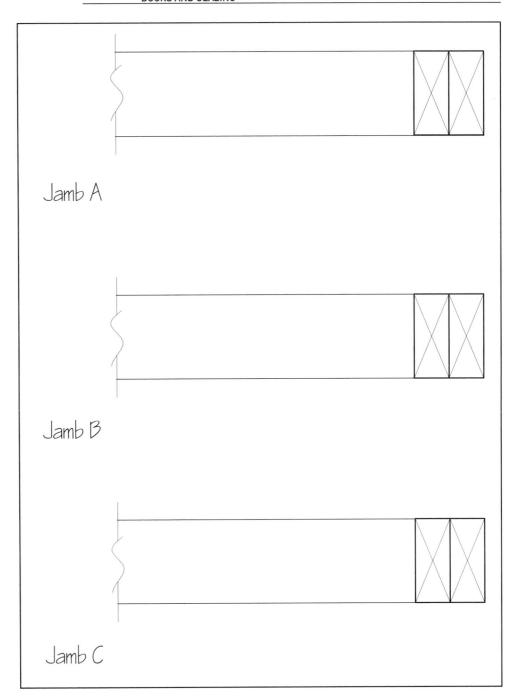

Jamb A

Jamb B

Jamb C

Hardware

1. On the following drawing, identify each of the indicated elements. Note that B and C are indicating the particular jamb side of the door.

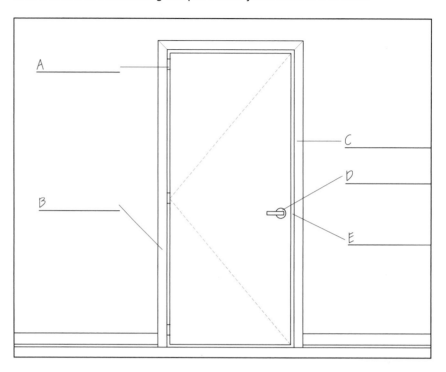

2. Visit a nearby hardware, lumber, or home improvement store. Examine hardware intended for residential use. Make note of comparative prices as well as features for various door knobs and lever handles. Note your perceptions of differences in the materials, craftsmanship, and tactile senses of quality. Be prepared to present and discuss your findings.

3. Visit nearby shopping malls, office buildings, or other commercial building types containing multiple occupants. Observe the main entry doors used by each occupant. For each door, note the material and approximate size (width and height). Make note of whether the doors use hinges or pivots to operate. If hinges, how many are located on each door? What type of hinges are they? If pivots, where are the pivots located? Discuss your observations and note patterns in the use of hinges versus pivots.

4. For required exit doors, the code states that "no special knowledge or ability" be necessary to operate the door. What does this mean in relation to door hardware?

_____

_____

_____

_____

_____

_____

_____

_____

_____

_____

_____

_____

_____

_____

CHAPTER SIX

Finish Work

Most projects include the design of elements including architectural woodwork, architectural metals, casework and cabinetry, and/or built-in furniture. Each of these categories of finish work for a project are included on construction documents in a detailed fashion, for inclusion as the project is built.

Architectural woodwork is the nonstructural woodwork, often decorative, that is a permanent part of a building. This may be the stile and rail paneling on a wall, a cornice around the top of a room, or casework. Wood interior finish components of a building, including moldings, window and door trim, cabinets, stairs, and mantels, can be millwork or finish carpentry.

Selection of the actual wood species will depend on aesthetic considerations of color, grain, and the ability to withstand denting. Each of wood's properties must be considered when using wood as a construction material. Aside from a consideration of suitability for a particular use and its distinct properties, the selection of a wood type is typically based on additional factors, including availability, sustainable practices, local practice or tradition, and comparative cost.

Each wood species has particular characteristics of color, grain, and pattern. The orientation of the cut relative to the direction of the growth rings determines a variety of lumber characteristics, such as dimensional stability and grain figure. Within a particular species of wood, the designer can select from a wide range of figure and grain patterns. Because wood is a natural material, grain patterns of any two trees are never exactly alike.

In the interior environment, metals are used in a variety of circumstances. Windows and doorframes as well as doors themselves are constructed of metal products. Stairs and railings are also commonly created of a variety of metal products. Nonstructural uses of metals in the interior environment include metals used as ceiling and wall finishes, room separators, and on custom designed furnishings and countertops. Each metal has specific properties related to hardness and finish, suitability for particular circumstances, and reactions to other metals.

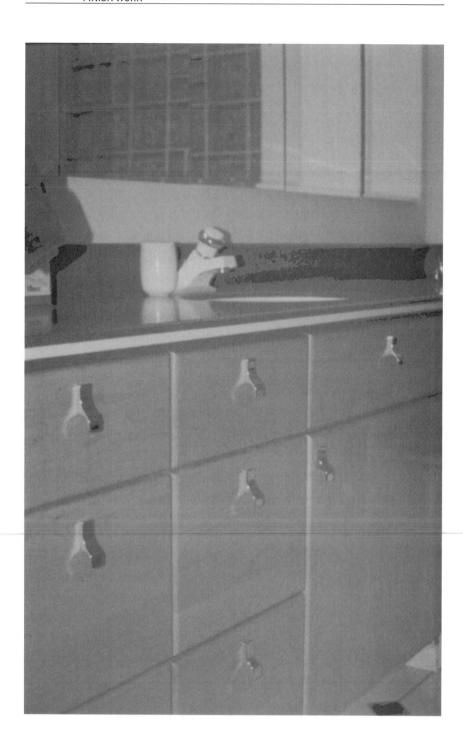

Casework and cabinets are found in virtually every project type. In residential projects, kitchens and baths provide a consistent opportunity to include cabinetry. The inclusion of casework often goes further than the kitchen and bath areas to include bookshelves, entertainment centers, and built-in dressers.

In commercial construction, a similar distribution of opportunities exists for casework and cabinetry. Whether storage in a conference room, display in a reception area, or workspace in a mailroom, casework and cabinetry play a role in the successful function and aesthetic of the space.

When designing and detailing casework and cabinetry, there are several decisions to make. Some of them affect the visual properties of the work; others affect some of the unseen but equally important functional characteristics. Main considerations in the design and selection of casework have to do with visual appearance, including materials and actual construction type, the budget for the project, maintenance and durability concerns (relating to materials, hinge styles, cleaning), and the accessories within.

Built-in furniture is furniture that is attached to the structure and becomes a permanent part of the building. Built-in furniture is custom-designed for the needs of individual projects. As such, built-in furniture becomes part of the architectural construction of the project and is treated as such on construction documents. Each of the considerations of moveable furniture comes into play in the design and representation of built-in furniture. Construction materials and methods determine the overall durability of the piece. Compatibility of materials, as well as the relationship between them, plays an important role. Fastener type and location, as well as the decision to reveal or hide fasteners, is determined by the overall design intent.

After reading the chapter, reviewing the illustrations and glossary entries, and reviewing associated web links, complete the following exercises.

Architectural Woodwork

1. In the space below, create an elevation or axonometric sketch at ¾" = 1' of a wall with stile and rail wood paneling. Identify each of the components included on the sketch, including cornice, chair rail, panel, stile, rail, and base.

Stile and Rail Wood Paneling

2. From a local lumber supplier, a reference book in your library, or internet resources provided by lumber manufacturers, select section profiles of various molding shapes to accomplish the following assignment:

Use the following template to draw a cornice in section that extends downward no further than 12" on the wall and extends no further than 8" outward on the ceiling. Use *five* different molding shapes to create this cornice. The drawing may be hard-lined (drafted) or soft-lined (freehand), but it must be to scale and utilize appropriate line weights for effective graphic communication.

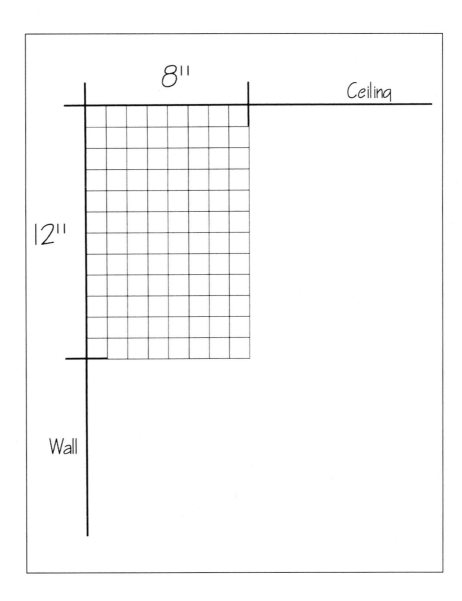

3. For this assignment, select the examples either from physical residential settings (use photographs of the spaces to supplement) or from examples in current design periodicals illustrating residential interior design (use copies of the photographs in the design periodicals to supplement). Select one example of the contemporary use of woodwork in a residential setting, as well as one example of a historical use of woodwork in a residential setting. Describe how the woodwork is used in a decorative mode in the two examples. Also describe any functional purposes of the woodwork in the two examples. Compare and contrast the two styles of use, including (but not limited to) a discussion of wood variety, color, relative sizes and placement, and the number of individual pieces required to achieve the final design. Supplement the written work with the images of the space.

4. Architectural woodwork may be quite ornate or straightforward in its application. The decision is typically related to the design intent or conceptual basis for the project. Select two published projects that are of similar types of commercial spaces (conference rooms, for example) but are very different in style and design. Compare and contrast the use of architectural woodwork in each. Discuss reasons you believe the designer made the choices shown. Include a representation of the two spaces used for this exercise with your written work.

Architectural Metals

1. Examine current (within the past 2 years) design periodicals (either architectural or interior design) to find an example of architectural metals used in a contemporary manner, and an example of architectural metals used in an historical or traditional setting. Describe the applications of architectural metals for the two settings. In addition to a description of the products used, be sure to include descriptions of the location of the use, whether it is applied to a surface or suspended, if it is used on the building components themselves or on movable furnishings. Fold the descriptions into a comparative analysis of the use of architectural metals in the examples you have found. Supplement the written work (250–500 words) with graphics (copies of the photographs or sketches).

2. Working alone or as a team, find as many examples of the interior use of architectural metals as possible in a two-hour period of time. Use the following sheets to record the placement of the metal, type of metal, and create an annotated thumbnail sketch of its use. Make additional copies of the following sheets as necessary.

Architectural Metals

PLACEMENT AND TYPE OF METAL

_____

_____

_____

PLACEMENT AND TYPE OF METAL

_____

_____

_____

Architectural Metals

PLACEMENT AND TYPE OF METAL

PLACEMENT AND TYPE OF METAL

Casework and Cabinetry

1. Scenario: You have designed a conference room for a toy manufacturer's main office. The client has requested wood shelves or other means of displaying current toys within this space. What factors will lead you as a designer to make the choice of designing millwork or finish carpentry for the displays?

_____

_____

_____

_____

_____

_____

_____

2. Use the kitchen plan shown on the CD-ROM for this exercise. Select a kitchen cabinet manufacturer and obtain their literature. Print out or recreate the drawing and note the pieces from the manufacturer necessary to accomplish the design. Be sure to include accessories and filler pieces. What challenges did you face during this exercise?

_____

_____

_____

_____

_____

_____

Built-In Furniture

1. Select an example of built-in furniture from either one of your own design projects, from a design periodical, or from observation of an actual space. Provide an image of the example you choose. On a separate sheet, sketch a section through the built-in furniture selected. (The sketch should be soft-line, to scale, and use appropriate line weights to effectively communicate your intentions.) Illustrate how this piece is connected to the wall, floor, or ceiling. Show finish materials, as well as the construction of the piece, using notes to describe each component.

2. Describe situations where built-in furniture may be more suitable than movable, free-standing furniture.

_____

_____

_____

_____

_____

_____

_____

_____

_____

_____

_____

_____

_____

_____

_____

_____

CHAPTER SEVEN
Integration of Lighting

Lighting is designed into a project for several reasons. The most basic functional consideration relates to task lighting, having an adequate amount and quality of light to accomplish certain tasks. Other lighting may be included to serve the purpose of accenting or highlighting certain architectural features or art pieces. Yet another purpose for integrating lighting in a project may be to create a certain level of ambient light in a space. The most remarkable designs typically include a combination of all three lighting functions.

Lighting to accomplish the functions mentioned may be attached to the surface of a wall or ceiling, may be recessed into a wall or ceiling, may be suspended from the ceiling, or may be structurally integrated into the design of a space. Each of these methods of attachment or inclusion requires consideration of the architectural surface and what lies behind it, the lamp to be provided and its characteristics, and any other special considerations due to luminaire or desired light action.

The most common integration is into the ceiling, where recessed lighting can support the appearance of a continuous, uninterrupted ceiling surface. Each of the components of the luminaire is housed above the ceiling surface, with the possible exception of the trim. If a recessed wall luminaire (sometimes found to light individual stairs, ramps, or other walking surfaces) is to be used, then the components are housed within the actual wall cavity.

When surface-mounted lighting is installed on a ceiling surface, the main consideration is with the depth of the fixture and the resulting head height available beneath it.

When surface-mounted lighting is installed on a wall surface, consideration must be given to the projection into the space. Especially in a corridor situation, wall sconces may create a situation where the projection interferes with the function of the space. In public spaces, the Americans with Disabilities Act (ADA) suggests that wall-mounted lighting occurring in the vertical zone from 27" up to 80" above the floor not project more than 4" into a space.

The height must accommodate the intended light action. For instance, indirect luminaires must be the appropriate distance from the ceiling so that light may bounce off, reflecting into the space. The remaining head height within the space must remain above minimums to avoid conflict. Lighting suspended above a fixed surface or object must have a mounting height to provide optimum light while avoiding direct glare possibilities.

The manner of suspension must then be considered. Most suspended luminaires are equipped with a certain type of suspension, whether it is cable, rod, or some other means.

When a high degree of attention is placed on the ceiling as a design element, often planes are lowered or raised to accentuate particular elements in the design. Where the ceiling changes, an excellent opportunity exists to provide integral lighting techniques as a part of the architecture rather than as a separate visible fixture.

Lighting may take the form of surface-mounted luminaires on the wall and/or ceiling within a space; or it may be provided through recessed or suspended luminaires. Lighting may also be provided through methods that are more structural in nature, for instance, that require a cove or soffits to be constructed or applied. Regardless of the actual method of providing light, the design of an effective lighting system must focus on several factors. These factors include the volume and shape of the space, the activities to occur within, and any special features to be accented.

Discussion of lighting in the chapter is subdivided into the major categories of recessed lighting, surface-mount lighting, suspended lighting, and special lighting construction. The chapter does not address the complex field of lighting design; rather, it focuses on the issues faced with the integration of various types of luminaires within a project. After reading the chapter, considering each of the integrated graphics, and reviewing the glossary items, answer or complete the following:

1. Select a recent project you have designed.

A. In 100 words, state your wishes for the lighting in terms of the effects the lighting will create or needs it will fulfill.

B. Overlay the plan, section, and a three-dimensional view of a space. Create a lighting design incorporating the effects of a variety of lighting forms, focusing for the first overlay only on the effects of the lighting, not on the actual method of accomplishing it. (Don't think of the actual luminaires at this point, only what effect the lighting will create within the space.)

C. On another overlay, propose luminaires that will accomplish the lighting effects you have proposed. Note on the sketches whether the lighting is recessed, surface-mounted, suspended, or structurally integrated.
 Be prepared to present and discuss this work.

2. Review the examples of cove and cornice lighting provided within the chapter. Observe the spaces around you in various buildings to locate additional examples of cove or cornice lighting. Select one example of cove and one example of cornice lighting and measure the particulars of the installation. On the following sheets, sketch a section through each example observed. Be sure to include notes to indicate material uses and type of lamp included (if that can be determined). Then answer the following questions following with regard to each example you have selected:

Cove Lighting: Sketch 1

A. How effective is the example you have selected in its contribution to the lighting quality within the space?

_____

_____

_____

B. How would you improve the luminaire?

_____

_____

_____

C. What materials are used in the construction of the integrated lighting?

_____

_____

_____

Cornice Lighting: Sketch 2

A. How effective is the example you have selected in its contribution to the lighting quality within the space?

_____

_____

_____

B. How would you improve the luminaire?

_____

_____

_____

C. What materials are used in the construction of the integrated lighting?

_____

_____

_____

3. Select an image from a recent (within the past 2 years) design periodical. Overlay the image with tracing paper and graphically analyze the lighting incorporated into the space. As part of the graphics you create over this image, show the output of light from the various sources. Are the sources hidden or visible?

_____

_____

Is the light spread from the sources in the form of a spot, is it linear in shape, or does the light form a large volume?

_____

_____

Show the shape from each source on the tracing paper and indicate the relative intensity of light emanating from that source. Use a scale of color or cross-hatching that illustrates the differences in intensity and shape. Refine your drawing by overlaying your analysis with additional traces with as much detail as necessary to communicate your findings. With notes pointing to the appropriate lighting, describe the lighting as recessed, surface mounted, suspended, or structurally integrated. Use this graphic to supplement a written description and analysis of the lighting shown in the image. In 250 words, describe what you think the designer was trying to accomplish with light in the design, the design attributes (characteristics) of the space shown in the image you have selected, and the contribution of each type of luminaire included. Supplement the written work with the graphic analysis. Include a copy of the original image from the design periodical.

4. Compile a minimum of four examples of suspended lighting "cut sheets" (manufacturers' technical literature). Compare the suspension techniques recommended for various ceiling materials. Describe with words and sketches, two of the recommended techniques.

Suspension Technique 1:

DESCRIPTION

Suspension Technique 2:

DESCRIPTION

_____

_____

_____

_____

_____

_____

_____

CHAPTER EIGHT

Integration of Building Systems

Earlier chapters have discussed the building, including structural systems as well as doors, windows, stairs, ramps, and partitions located within. Chapter 8, "Integration of Building Systems," presents general information regarding the mechanical, electrical, plumbing, and fire protection systems as they affect decisions made by the interior designer. Understanding the implications and physical presence of each of these systems presents opportunities to maximize the efficiency of design decisions at a reasonable cost to the client.

Mechanical Systems

The mechanical system for a building may provide heat, cooling, ventilation, and air treatment. Depending on the type of building construction and the size and use of the occupancies within, the mechanical system may involve a number of components with hefty space requirements. In large commercial buildings, equipment located within mechanical spaces may be supplemented with components located on the roof or on the ground adjacent to the building. In residential buildings, most equipment fits within a small mechanical space and may be supplemented by exterior units.

Regardless of the type of mechanical system designed for a building, the building's thermal efficiency relies on additional features. The thermal envelope of the building is an important attribute. The amount and type of insulation, as well as efficiency of doors and windows, affect the size and efficiency of the mechanical system to heat, cool, or otherwise condition the habitable space. Effective solar orientation of windows in small buildings may lessen the heat required to be supplied by a mechanical system.

1. On a set of mechanical plans, the room names are shown with room numbers, just as on the architectural or interior design plans. This allows easy reference and relation of spaces in the building. On the portion of a mechanical plan included on the CD-ROM, answer the following questions:

A. What size of rectangular duct feeds Room 102 BOARD OF EDUCATION? _____" wide by _____" high

B. What size of ducts feed the two diffusers in Room 102 BOARD OF EDUCATION?
_____"

C. Are the ducts that feed the two diffusers in Room 102 Board of Education rectangular or round?

_____

2. For a given space (you may select the space as your classroom, library, or other) speculate what the mechanical system might be by observing several items: Are there registers or diffusers that distribute air to the space?

_____

If yes, where are they located, and are they on the ceiling, floor, or wall plane? (Draw a plan sketch of the space showing the locations.) Estimate or measure the size of the registers or diffusers:

_____" × _____"
_____" × _____"
_____" × _____"

Are there radiators within the space? If yes, where are they located? Measure the width, depth, and height of any radiators and record here:

_____" × _____" × _____"
_____" × _____" × _____"
_____" × _____" × _____"

Do any other elements provide heating or cooling within the space? If so, describe them:

_____

_____

_____

_____

Electrical Systems

Electrical power is supplied to a building site at a high voltage and then transformed to a usable voltage. Power is supplied for lighting, equipment, and convenience outlets. Depending on the use of the spaces within the building, that voltage may be 120/240v or 208/440v. Residential spaces utilize 120/240v power, whereas many commercial occupancies utilize 208/440v power for efficiency.

From the electrical entrance into the building, the power must be distributed to the end uses. This is accomplished through the use of panels containing control and protection devices (either circuit breakers or fuses). From the panels, the power is distributed to the end uses via wiring. Individual wires must be protected to some degree in every type of construction. In residential construction, this protection occurs through the wrap of each wire in plastic; the wire grouping is then sheathed within a plastic sleeve. In commercial construction, the wires are then also located within conduit.

1. Search the floor plan located on the CD-ROM for information that will help you with the exercises below.

Print the floor plan onto a sheet of 8½" × 11" paper and highlight each of the electric receptacles.

What is the maximum spacing for convenience outlets in the rooms shown? (Name the room and maximum distance.)

2. In your place of residence measure where electrical receptacles are located around the room (note the distance from corners and the space between the receptacles). Draw a sketch and illustrate these locations and measurements. What is the height of the electrical receptacles off of the floor surface? _____" to the centerline.

Note where light switches are located in the same room. What is the height of the light switches off of the floor surface? _____" to the centerline. How far from a door jamb or opening is the light switch located? _____" to the centerline. Why do you think the light switch is not closer to the doorjamb or opening?

_____

_____

_____

_____

_____

_____

Plumbing Systems

Plumbing systems are divided into the supply system and the drainage or waste system. Requirements for each system are quite different, their difference based on the fact that the supply system is under pressure while the drainage system works through gravity.

Search the plumbing drawings located on the CD-ROM for information to answer the following questions or to conduct the following activities: Describe which, if any, of the walls shown on the Plumbing plan are "wet" walls.

_____

_____

_____

_____

_____

_____

Locate hot water and cold water lines. How are the hot water lines designated?

_____

How are the cold water lines designated?

_____

Fire Protection Systems

Fire protection is an umbrella term that covers all aspects of detecting, alarming, and extinguishing fires within buildings.

Use the upper floor plan shown on the CD-ROM to indicate where smoke detectors would need to be located according to the 2000 International Building Code. Describe where smoke detectors would be required on this floor plan, including room names.

_____

_____

_____

_____

_____

_____

_____

_____

_____

_____